Lord Kitchener

G. K. Chesterton

Horatio Herbert Kitchener was Irish by birth but English by extraction, being born in County Kerry, the son of an English colonel. The fanciful might see in this first and accidental fact the presence of this simple and practical man amid the more mystical western problems and dreams which were very distant from his mind, an element which clings to all his career and gives it an unconscious poetry. He had many qualities of the epic hero, and especially this—that he was the last man in the world to be the epic poet. There is something almost provocative to superstition in the way in which he stands at every turn as the symbol of the special trials and the modern transfiguration of England; from this moment when he was born among the peasants of Ireland to the moment when he died upon the sea, seeking at the other end of the world the other great peasant civilisation of Russia. Yet at each of these symbolic moments he is, if not as unconscious as a symbol, then as silent as a symbol; he is speechless and supremely significant, like an ensign or a flag. The superficial picturesqueness of his life, at least, lies very much in this—that he was like a hero condemned by fate to act an allegory.

We find this, for instance, in one of the very first and perhaps one of the most picturesque of all the facts that are recorded or reported of him. As a youth, tall, very shy and quiet, he was only notable for intellectual interests of the soberest and most methodical sort, especially for the close study of mathematics. This also, incidentally, was typical enough, for his work in Egypt and the Soudan, by which his fame was established, was based wholly upon such calculations. It was not merely mathematical but literally geometrical. His work bore the same relation to Gordon's that a rigid mathematical diagram bears to a rough pencil sketch on which it is based. Yet the student thus bent on the strictest side of his profession, studying it at Woolwich and entering the Engineers as the most severely scientific branch of the army, had as a first experience of war something so romantic that it has been counted incredible, yet something so relevant to the great reality of to-day that it might have been made up centuries after his death, as a myth is made up about a god. He happened to be in France in the most tragic hour that France has ever known or, please God, will ever know. She was bearing alone the weight of that alien tyranny, of that hopeless and almost lifeless violence, which the other nations have since found to be the worst of all the terrors which God tolerates in this world. She trod that winepress alone; and of the peoples there were none to help her. In 1870 the Prussian had already encircled Paris, and General Chanzy was fighting against enormous odds to push northwards to its relief, when his army was joined by the young and silent traveller from England. All that was in Kitchener's mind or motives will perhaps never be known. France was still something of an ideal of civilisation for many of the more generous English gentry. Prussia was never really an ideal for anybody, even the Prussians, and mere success, which could not make her an ideal, had not yet calamitously made her a model. There was in it also, no doubt, a touch of the schoolboy who runs away to sea—that touch of the schoolboy without the sense of which the staidest Englishman will always be inexplicable. But considered historically there is something strangely moving about the incident—the fact that Kitchener was a French soldier almost before he was an English one. As Hannibal was dedicated in boyhood to war against the eagles of Rome, Kitchener was dedicated, almost in boyhood, to war against the eagles of Germany. Romance came to this realist, whether by impulse or by accident, like a wind from without, as first love will come to the woman-hater. He was already, both by fate and choice, something more than he had meant to be. The mathematician, we might almost say the calculating boy, was already gambling in the highest lottery which led to the highest and most historic loss. The engineer devoted to discipline was already a free lance, because already a knight-errant.

He returned to England to continue his comparatively humdrum order of advancement; and the next call that came to him was of a strangely different and yet also of a strangely significant kind. The Palestine Exploration Fund sent him with another officer to conduct topographical and antiquarian investigations in a country where practical exertions are always relieved against a curiously incongruous background—as if they were setting up telegraph-posts through the Garden of Eden or opening a railway station at the New Jerusalem. But the contrast between antiquity and modernity was not the only one; there was still the sort of contrast that can be a collision. Kitchener was almost immediately to come in contact with what was to be, in various aspects, the problem of his life—the modern fanaticisms of the Near East. There is an English proverb which asks whether the mountain goes to Mahomet or he to the mountain, and it may be a question whether his religion be the cause or the effect of a certain spirit, vivid and yet strangely negative, which dwells in such deserts. Walking among the olives of Gaza or looking on the Philistine plain, such travellers may well feel that they are treading on cold volcanoes, as empty as the mountains of the moon. But the mountain of Mahomet is not yet an extinct volcano.

Kitchener, in these first days of seemingly mild and minute duties, was early aware of it. At Safed, in the Galilean hills, his small party had found itself surrounded by an Arab mob, stricken suddenly mad with emotions unintelligible to the political mobs of the West. He was himself wounded, but, defending himself as best he could with a walking-stick, not only saved his own life but that of his fellow-officer, Lieutenant Conder, who had been beaten to the earth with an Arab club. He continued his work indeed with prosaic pertinacity, and developed in the survey of the Holy Land all that almost secretive enthusiasm for detail which lasted all his life. Of the most famous English guide-book he made the characteristic remark, "Where Murray has seven names I have a hundred and sixteen." Most men, in speaking or writing of such a thing, would certainly have said "a hundred." It is characteristic of his type that he did not even think in round numbers. But there was in him, parallel to this almost arithmetical passion, another quality which is, in a double sense, the secret of his life. For it was the cause of at least half his success; and yet he very successfully concealed it—especially from his admirers.

The paradox of all this part of his life lies in this—that, destined as he was to be the greatest enemy of Mahomedanism, he was quite exceptionally a friend of Mahomedans. He had been first received in that land, so to speak, with a blow on the head with a club; he was destined to break the sword of the last Arab conqueror, to wreck his holy city and treat all the religious traditions of it with a deliberate desecration which has often been held oppressive and was undoubtedly ruthless. Yet with the individual Moslem he had a sort of natural brotherhood which has never been explained. Had it been shown by a soldier of the Crusades, it would have been called witchcraft. In this, as in many other cases, the advance of a larger enlightenment prevents us from calling it anything. There was mixed with it, no doubt, the deep Moslem admiration for mere masculinity, which has probably by its exaggeration permitted the Moslem subordination of women. But Kitchener (who was himself accused, rightly or wrongly, of a disdain for women) must have himself contributed some other element to the strangest of international sympathies. Whatever it was, it must be constantly kept in mind as running parallel to his scientific industry and particularity; for it was these two powers, used systematically for many years before the event, that prepared the ground for the overthrow of that wild papacy and wandering empire which so long hung in the desert, like a mirage to mislead and to destroy.

Kitchener was called away in 1878 to similar surveying duties in Cyprus, and afterwards in Anatolia, where the same faculty obtained him a firman, making him safe in all the Holy Cities of Islam. He also dealt much with the Turkish fugitives fleeing from the Russian guns to Erzerum—whither, so long after, the guns were to follow. But it is with his later summons to Egypt that we feel he has returned to the theatre of the great things of his life. It is not necessary in this rough sketch to discuss the rights and wrongs or the general international origin of the British occupation of Egypt; the degree of praise or blame to be given to the Khedive, who was the nominal ruler, or to Arabi, the Nationalist leader, who for a time seized the chief power in his place. Kitchener's services in the operations by which Arabi was defeated were confined to some reconnaissance work immediately preceding the bombardment of Alexandria; and the problem with which his own personality became identified was not that of the Government of Egypt, but of the more barbaric power beyond, by which Egypt, and any powers ruling it, came to be increasingly imperilled. And what advanced him rapidly to posts of real responsibility in the new politics of the country was the knowledge he already had of wilder men and more mysterious forces than could be found in Egyptian courts or even Egyptian camps. It was the combination, of which we have already spoken, of detailed experience and almost eccentric sympathy. In practice it was his knowledge of Arabic, and still more his knowledge of Arabs.

There is in Islam a paradox which is perhaps a permanent menace. The great creed born in the desert creates a kind of ecstasy out of the very emptiness of its own land, and even, one may say, out of the emptiness of its own theology. It affirms, with no little sublimity, something that is not merely the singleness but rather the solitude of God. There is the same extreme simplification in the solitary figure of the Prophet; and yet this isolation perpetually reacts into its own opposite. A void is made in the heart of Islam which has to be filled up again and again by a mere repetition of the revolution that founded it. There are no sacraments; the only thing that can happen is a sort of apocalypse, as unique as the end of the world; so the apocalypse can only be repeated and the world end again and again. There are no priests; and yet this equality can only breed a multitude of lawless prophets almost as numerous as priests. The very dogma that there is only one Mahomet produces an endless procession of Mahomets. Of these the mightiest in modern times were the man whose name was Ahmed, and whose more famous title was the Mahdi; and his more ferocious successor Abdullahi, who was generally known as the Khalifa. These great fanatics, or great creators of fanaticism, succeeded in making a militarism almost as famous and formidable as that of the Turkish Empire on whose frontiers it hovered, and in spreading a reign of terror such as can seldom be organised except by civilisation. With Napoleonic suddenness and success the Mahdist hordes had fallen on the army of Hicks Pasha, when it left its camp at Omdurman, on the Nile opposite Khartoum, and had cut it to pieces in a fashion incredible. They had established at Omdurman their Holy City, the Rome of their nomadic Roman Empire. Towards that terrible place many adventurous men, like poor Hicks, had gone and were destined to go. The sands that encircled it were like that entrance to the lion's cavern in the fable, towards which many footprints pointed, and from which none returned.

The last of these was Gordon, that romantic and even eccentric figure of whom so much might be said. Perhaps the most essential thing to say of him here is that fortune once again played the artist in sending such a man, at once as the leader and the herald of a man like Kitchener; to show the way and to make the occasion; to be a sacrifice and a signal for vengeance. Whatever else there was about Gordon, there was about him the air not only of a hero, but of the hero of a tragedy. Something Oriental in his own mysticism, something most of his countrymen would have called moonshine, something perverse in his courage, something childish and beautiful in that perversity, marked him out as the man who walks to doom—the man who in a hundred poems or fables goes up to a city to be crucified. He had gone to Khartoum to arrange the withdrawal of the troops from the Soudan, the Government having decided, if possible, to live at peace with the new Mahdist dictatorship; and he went through the deserts almost as solitary as a bird, on a journey as lonely as his end. He was cut off and besieged in Khartoum by the Mahdist armies, and fell with the falling city. Long before his end he had been in touch with Kitchener, now of the Egyptian Intelligence Department, and weaving very carefully a vast net of diplomacy and strategy in which the slayers of Gordon were to be taken at last.

A well-known English journalist, Bennet Burleigh, wandering near Dongola, fell into conversation with an Arab who spoke excellent English, and who, with a hospitality highly improper in a Moslem, produced two bottles of claret for his entertainment. The name of this Arab was Kitchener; and the two bottles were all he had. The journalist obtained, along with the claret, his first glimpse of the great and extraordinary schemes with which Kitchener was already working to avenge the comrade who had fallen in Khartoum. This part of the work was as personal as that of a private detective plotting against a private murderer in a modern detective story. Kitchener had learned to speak the Arab tongue not only freely but sociably. He wore the Arab dress and fell into the Arab type of courtesy so effectively that even his blue northern eyes did not betray him. Above all, he sympathised with the Arab character; and in a thousand places sprinkled over the map of North-East Africa he made friends for himself and therefore enemies for the Mahdi. This was the first and superficially the most individual of the converging plans which were to checkmate the desert empire; and its effects were very far-reaching. Again and again, in subsequent years, when the missionaries of the Mahdist religion pushed northward, they found themselves entangled among tribes which the English power had not so much conquered as converted. The legend of the great Prophet encountered something more elusive than laws or military plans; it encountered another legend—an influence which also carried the echoes of the voice of a man. The Ababdeh Arabs, it was said, made a chain across the desert, which the new and awful faith could not pass. The Mudir of Dongola was on the point of joining the ever-victorious Prophet of Omdurman. Kitchener, clad as an Arab, went out almost alone to speak with him. What passed, perhaps, we can never tell; but before his guest had even left him the Mudir flew to arms, fell upon the Prophet's hosts at Korti, and drove them before him.

The second and superficially more solid process of preparation is much better known. It was the education of the native Egyptian army. It is not necessary to swallow all the natural jingoism of English journalism in order to see something truly historic about the English officer's work with the Fellaheen, or native race of Egypt. For centuries they had lain as level as the slime of the Nile, and all the conquerors in the chronicles of men had passed over them like a pavement. Though professing the challenging creed of the Moslems, they seem to have reached something like the pessimist patience of the Hindoos. To have turned this slime once more into a human river, to have lifted this pavement once more into a human rampart or barricade, is not a small thing, nor a thing that could possibly be done even by mere power, still less by mere money—and this Kitchener and his English companions certainly did. There must have been something much more than a mere cynical severity in "organisation" in the man who did it. There must be something more than a mere commercial common-sense in the nation in whose name it was done. It is easy enough, with sufficient dulness and greed of detail, to "organise" anything or anybody.

It is easy enough to make people obey a bugle (or a factory hooter) as the Prussian soldiers obey a bugle. But it is no such trumpet that makes possible the resurrection of the dead.

The success of this second of the three converging designs of Kitchener, the making of a new Egyptian army, was soon seen in the expedition against Dongola. It had been foreshadowed in a successful defence of Suakin, in which Kitchener was wounded; a defence against Osman Digna, perhaps the first of the Mahdist generals whose own strongholds were eventually stormed at Gemaizeh; and in the victory at Toski, where fell the great warrior Wad el Njume, whose strategy had struck down both Hicks and Gordon. But the turn of the tide was Dongola. In 1892 General, now Lord Grenfell, who had been Sirdar, or Commander-in-Chief of the Egyptian Army, and ordered the advance at Toski, retired and left his post vacant. The great public servant known latterly as Lord Cromer had long had his eye on Kitchener and the part he had played, even as a young lieutenant, in the new military formation of the Fellaheen. He was now put at the head of the whole new army; and the first work that fell to him was leading the new expedition. In three days after the order was received the force started at nightfall and marched southward into the night. The detail is something more than picturesque; for on all accounts of that formidable attack on the Mahdi's power a quality of darkness rests like a kind of cloud. It was, for one thing, a surprise attack and a very secret one, so that the cloud was as practical as a cloak; but it was also the re-entrance of a territory which an instinct has led the English to call the Dark Continent even under its blazing noon. There vast distances alone made a veil like that of darkness, and there the lives of Gordon and Hicks and hundreds more had been swallowed up in an ancient silence. Perhaps we cannot guess to-day, after the colder completion of Kitchener's work, what it meant for those who went on that nocturnal march; who crept up in two lines, one along the river and the other along an abandoned railway track, moving through the black night; and in the black night encamped, and waited for the rising of the moon. Anyhow, the tale told of it strikes this note, especially in one touch of what can only be called a terrible triviality. I mean the reference to the new noise heard just before day-break, revealing the nearness of the enemy: the dreadful drum of Islam, calling for prayer to an awful God—a God not to be worshipped by the changing and sometimes cheerful notes of harp or organ, but only by the drum that maddens by mere repetition.

But the third of Kitchener's lines of approach remains to consider. The surprise attack, which captured the riverside village of Firket, had eventually led, in spite of storms that warred on the advance like armies, and in one place practically wiped out a brigade, to the fall of Dongola itself. But Dongola was not the high place of the enemy; it was not there that Gordon died or that Abdullahi was still alive. Far away up the dark river were the twin cities of the tragedy, the city of the murder and the city of the murderer. It was in relation to this fixed point of fact that Kitchener's next proceeding is seen to be supremely characteristic. He was so anxious to do one thing that he was cautious about doing it. He was more concerned to obtain a success than to appear to deserve it; he did not want a moral victory, but a mathematical certainty. So far from following up the dash in the dark, upon Firket or Dongola, with more romantic risks, he decided not to advance on the Mahdi's host a minute faster than men could follow him building a railway. He created behind him a colossal causeway of communications, going out alone into wastes where there was and had been no other mortal trace or track. The engineering genius of Girouard, a Canadian, designed and developed it with what was, considering the nature of the task, brilliant rapidity; but by the standards of desert warfare it must have seemed that Kitchener and his English made war as slowly as grass grows or orchards bear fruit. The horsemen of Araby, darting to and fro like swallows, must have felt as if they were menaced by the advance of a giant snail. But it was a snail that left a shining track unknown to those sands; for the first time since Rome decayed something was being made there that could remain. The effect of this growing road, one might almost say this living road, began to be felt. Mahmoud, the Mahdist military leader, fell back from Berber, and gathered his hosts more closely round the sacred city on the Nile. Kitchener, making another night march up the Atbara river, stormed the Arab camp and took Mahmoud prisoner. Then at last he moved finally up the western bank of the Nile and came in sight of Omdurman. It is somewhat of a disproportion to dwell on the fight that followed and the fall of the great city. The fighting had been done already, and more than half of it was working; fighting a long fight against the centuries, against ages of sloth and the great sleep of the desert, where there had been nothing but visions, and against a racial decline that men had accepted as a doom. On the following Sunday a memorial service for Charles Gordon was held in the place where he was slain.

The fact that Kitchener fought with rails as much as with guns rather fixed from this time forward the fashionable view of his character. He was talked of as if he were himself made of metal, with a head filled not only with calculations but with clockwork. This is symbolically true, in so far as it means that he was by temper what he was by trade, an engineer. He had conquered the Mahdi, where many had failed to do so. But what he had chiefly conquered was the desert—a great and greedy giant. He brought Cairo to Khartoum; we might say that he brought London or Liverpool with him to the gates of the strange city of Omdurman. Some parts of his action supported, even regrettably, the reputation of rigidity. But if any admirer had, in this hour of triumph, been staring at him as at a stone sphinx of inflexible fate, that admirer would have been very much puzzled by the next passage of his life. Kitchener was something much more than a machine; for in the mind, as much as in the body, flexibility is far more masculine than inflexibility.

A situation developed almost instantly after his victory in which he was to show that he was a diplomatist as well as a soldier. At Fashoda, a little farther up the Nile, he found something more surprising, and perhaps more romantic, than the wildest dervish of the desert solitudes. A French officer, and one of the most valiant and distinguished of French officers, Major Marchand, had penetrated to the place with the pertinacity of a great explorer, and seemed prepared to hold it with all the unselfish arrogance of a patriot. It is said that the Frenchman not only welcomed Kitchener in the name of France, but invited him, with courteous irony, to partake of vegetables grown on the spot, a symbol of stable occupation. The story, if it be true, is admirably French; for it reveals at once the wit and the peasant. But the humour of the Englishman was worthily equal to the wit of the Frenchman; and it was humour of that sane sort which we call good humour. Political papers in pacific England and France raved and ranted over the crisis, responsible journals howled with jingoism; but through it all, until the moment when the French agreed to retire, the two most placable and even sociable figures were the two grim tropical travellers and soldiers who faced each other on the burning sands of Fashoda. As we see them facing each other, we have again the vague sense of a sign or a parable which runs through this story. For they were to meet again long afterwards as allies, when both were leading their countrymen against the great enemy in the Great War.

Something of the same shadow of prophecy is perhaps the deepest memory left by the last war of Kitchener before the greatest. After further activities in Egypt and the Soudan, of which the attempt to educate the Fellaheen by the Gordon Memorial College was the most remarkable, he was abruptly summoned to South Africa to be the right hand of Lord Roberts in the war then being waged against the Boers. He conducted the opening of the determining battle of Paardeberg, and was typically systematic in covering the half-conquered country with a system of block-houses and enclosures like a diagram of geometry. But to-day, and for many reasons, Englishmen will think first of the last scene of that war. When Botha and the Boer Generals surrendered to Kitchener, there was the same goodwill among the soldiers to contrast with the ill-will of the journalists. Botha also became almost a friend; and Botha also was to be in the far future an ally, smiting the German in Africa as Kitchener smote him in Europe. There was the same hint of prophecy about the war that ended at Vereeniging as about that other war that so nearly began at Fashoda. It seemed almost as if God were pitting his heroes against each other in tournament, before they all rode together against the heathen pouring upon them out of Germany.

It is with that name of Germany that this mere skeleton of the facts must end. After the South African War Kitchener had been made Commander-in-Chief in India, where he effected several vital changes, notably the emancipation of that office from the veto of the Military Member of the Council of the Viceroy, and where he showed once more, in his dealings with the Sepoys, that obscure yet powerful sympathy with the mysterious intellect of the East. Thence he had been again shifted to Egypt; but the next summons that came to him swallowed up all these things. A short time after war broke out with Germany he was made Minister of War, and held that post until the dark season when he set out on a mission to Russia, which never reached its goal. But when his ship went down he had already done a work and registered a change in England, with some words about which this sketch may well conclude. Journalistic attacks were indeed made upon him, but in writing for a foreign reader I pass them by. In such a place I will not say even of the meanest of Englishmen what they were not ashamed to say of one of the greatest. In his new work he was not only a very great man, but one dealing with very great things; and perhaps his most historic moment was when he broke his customary silence about the deeper emotions of life, and became the mouthpiece of the national horror at the German fashion of fighting, which he declared to have left a stain upon the whole profession of arms. For, by a movement unusually and unconsciously dramatic, he chose that moment to salute across the long stretch of years the comparative chivalry and nobility of his dead enemies of the Soudan, and to announce that in the heart of Europe, in learned academies and ordered government offices, there had appeared a lunacy so cruel and unclean that the maddest dervish dead in the desert had a right to disdain it where he lay.

Kitchener, like other Englishmen of his type, made his name outside England and even outside Europe. But it was in England, and after his return to England, that he did what will perhaps make his name most permanent in history. That return to England was indeed as symbolic as his last and tragic journey to Russia. Both will stand as symbols of the deepest things which are moving mankind in the Great War. In truth the whole of that great European movement which we call the cause of the Allies is in itself a homeward journey. It is a return to native and historic ideals, after an exile in the howling wilderness of the political pessimism and cynicism of Prussia. After his great adventures in Africa and Asia, the Englishman has re-discovered Europe; and in the very act of discovering Europe, the Englishman has at last discovered England. The revelation of the forces still really to be found in England itself, when all is said that can possibly or plausibly be said against English commercialism and selfishness, was the last work of Lord Kitchener. He was the embodiment of an enormous experience which has passed through Imperialism and reached patriotism. He had been the supreme figure of that strange and sprawling England which lies beyond England; which carries the habits of English clubs and hotels into the solitudes of the Nile or up the passes of the Himalayas, and is infinitely ignorant of things infinitely nearer home. For this type of Englishman Cairo was nearer than Calais. Yet the typical figure which we associated with such places as Cairo was destined before he died to open again the ancient gate of Calais and lead in a new and noble fashion the return of England to Europe. The great change for which his countrymen will probably remember him longest was what we should call in England the revolution of the New Armies.

It is almost impossible to express how great a revolution it was so as to convey its dimensions to the citizens of any other great European country where military service has long been the rule and not the exception, where the people itself is only the army in mufti. In its mere aspect to the eye it was something like an invasion by a strange race. The English professional soldier of our youth had been conspicuous not only by his red coat but by his rarity. When rare things become common they do not become commonplace. The memory of their singularity is still strong enough to give them rather the appearance of a prodigy, as anyone can realise by imagining an army of hunchbacks or a city of one-eyed men. The English soldier had indeed been respected as a patriotic symbol, but rather as a priest or a prince can be a symbol, as being the exception and not the rule. A child was taken to see the soldier outside Buckingham Palace almost as he was taken to see the King driving out of Buckingham Palace. Hence the first effect of the enlargement of the armies was something almost like a fairy-tale—almost as if the streets were crowded with kings, walking about and wearing crowns of gold. This merely optical vision of the revolution was but the first impression of a reality equally vast and new. The first levies which came to be called popularly Kitchener's Army, because of the energy and inspiration with which he set himself to their organisation, consisted entirely of volunteers. It was not till long after the whole face of England had been transformed by this mobilisation that the Government resorted to compulsion to bring in a mere margin of men. Save for the personality of Kitchener, the new militarism of England came wholly and freely from the English. While it was as universal as a tax, it was as spontaneous as a riot. But it is obvious that to produce so large and novel an effect out of the mere psychology of a nation, apart from its organisation, was something which required tact as well as decision: and it is this which illustrated a side of the English general's character without which he may be, and indeed has been, wholly misunderstood.

It is of the nature of national heroes of Kitchener's type that their admirers are unjust to them. They would have been better appreciated if they had been less praised. When a soldier is turned into an idol there seems an unfortunate tendency to turn him into a wooden idol, like the wooden figure of Hindenburg erected by the ridiculous authorities of Berlin. In a more moderate and metaphorical sense there has been an unfortunate tendency to represent Kitchener as strong by merely representing him as stiff—to suggest that he was made of wood and not of steel. There are two maxims, which have been, I believe, the mottoes of two English families, both of which are boasts but each the contrary of the other. The first runs, "You can break me, but you cannot bend me"; and the second, "You can bend me, but you cannot break me." With all respect to whoever may have borne it, the first is the boast of the barbarian and therefore of the Prussian; the second is the boast of the Christian and the civilised man—that he is free and flexible, yet always returns to his true position, like a tempered sword. Now too much of the eulogy on a man like Kitchener tended to praise him not as a sword but as a poker. He happened to rise into his first fame at a time when much of the English Press and governing class was still entirely duped by Germany, and to some extent judged everything by a Bismarckian test of blood and iron. It tended to neglect the very real disadvantages, even in practical life, which lie upon the man of blood and iron, as compared with the man of blood and bone. It is one grave disadvantage, for instance, that if a man made of iron were to break his bones, they would not heal. In other words, the Prussian Empire, with all its perfections and efficiencies, has one notable defect—that it is a dead thing. It does not draw its life from any primary human religion or poetry; it does not grow again from within. And being a dead thing, it suffers also from having no nerves to give warning or reaction; it reads no danger signals; it has no premonitions; about its own spiritual doom its sentinels are deaf and all its spies are blind. On the other hand, the British Empire, with all its blunders and bad anomalies, to which I am the last person to be blind, has one noticeable advantage—that it is a living thing. It is not that it makes no mistakes, but it knows it has made them, as the living hand knows when it has touched hot iron. That is exactly what a hand of iron would not know; and that is exactly the error in the German ideal of a hand of iron. No candid critic of England can read its history fairly and fail to see a certain flexibility and self-modification; illiberal policies followed by liberal ones; men failing in something and succeeding in something else; men sent to do one thing and being wise enough to do another; the human power of the living hand to draw back. As it happens, Kitchener was extraordinarily English in this lively and vital moderation. And it is to be feared that the more German idealisation of him, in the largely unenlightened England before the war, has already done some harm to his reputation, and in missing what was particularly English has missed what was particularly interesting.

Lord Kitchener was personally a somewhat silent man; and his social conventions were those of the ordinary English officer, especially the officer who has lived among Orientals—conventions which in any case tend in the direction of silence. He also really had, and to an extent of which some people complained, a certain English embarrassment about making all his purposes clear, especially before they were clear to himself. He probably liked to think a thing out in his own way and therefore at his own time, which was not always the time at which people thought they had a right to question him. In this way it is true of him, as of such another strong man as the Irish patriot Parnell, that his very simplicity had an effect of secrecy. But it is a complete error about him, as it was a complete error about Parnell, to suppose that he took the Prussian pose of disdaining and disregarding everybody; that he settled everything in solitary egoism; that he was a Superman too self-sufficing to listen to friends and too philosophical to listen to reason. It will be noted that every crisis of his life that is lit up by history contradicts the colours of this picture. He could not only take counsel with his friends, but he was abnormally successful in taking counsel with his foes. It is notable that whenever he came in personal contact with a great captain actually or potentially in arms against him, the result was not a mere collision but a mutual comprehension. He established the friendliest relations with the chivalrous and adventurous Marchand, standing on the deadly debatable land of Fashoda. He established equally friendly relations with the Boer generals, gathered under the dark cloud of national disappointment and defeat. In all such instances, so far as his individuality could count, it is clear that he acted as a moderate and, in the universal sense, as a liberal. The results and the records of those who met him in such hours are quite sufficient to prove that he did not leave the impression of a Prussian arrogance. If he was silent, his silence must have been more friendly, I had almost said more convivial, than many men's conversation. But on the larger platform of the European War, this quiet but unique gift of open-mindedness and intellectual hospitality was destined to do two very decisive things, which may profoundly affect history. In the first he dealt with the more democratic and even revolutionary elements in England; and in the second he represents a very real change that has passed over the English traditions about Russia.

Personally, as has already been noted, Lord Kitchener never was and never pretended to be anything more or less than the good military man, and by the time of the Great War he was already an elderly military man. The type has much the same standards and traditions in all European countries; but in England it is, if anything, a little more traditional, for the very reason that the army has been something separate, professional, and relatively small—a sort of club. The military man was all the more military because the nation was not military. Such a man is inevitably conservative in his views, conventional in his manners, and simplifies the problem of patriotism to a single-eyed obedience. When he took over the business of raising the first levies for the present war he was confronted with the problem of the English Trades Unions—the very last problem in the world which one could reasonably expect such a man to understand. And yet he did understand it; he was perhaps the only person in the governing class who did. If it be hard to explain to the richer classes in England, it is almost impossible to explain to any classes in any other country, because the English situation is largely unique. There is the same difficulty as we have already found in describing how vast and even violent a transformation scene the growth of the great army appeared; it has been almost impossible to describe it to the chief conscript countries, which take a great army for granted. The key to the parallel problem of the Trades Unions is simply this—that England is the only European country that is practically industrial and nothing else. Trades Unions can never play such a part in countries where the masses live on the land; such masses always have some status and support—yes, even if they are serfs. The status of the English workman is not in the earth; it is, so to speak, in the air—in a scaffolding of artificial abstractions, a framework of rules and rights, of verbal bargains or paper resolutions. If he loses this, he becomes nothing so human or homely as a slave. Rather he becomes a wild beast, a sort of wandering vermin with no place in the state at all. It would be necessary to explain this, and a great deal more which cannot possibly be explained here, before we could measure the enormity of the enigma facing the British official who had to propose to the English the practical suspension of the Trades Unions. To this must be added the fact that the Unions, already national institutions, had just lately been in a ferment with new and violent doctrines: Syndicalists had invoked them as the future seats of government; historical speculators had seen in them the return to the great Christian Guilds of the Middle Ages; a more revolutionary Press had appeared to champion them; gigantic strikes had split the country in every direction. Anyone would have said that under these circumstances the very virtues and attainments of

Kitchener would at least make it fairly certain that he would quarrel with the Trades Unions. It soon became apparent that the one man who was not going to quarrel with the Trades Unions was Kitchener. Politicians and parliamentary leaders, supposed actually to be elected by the working classes, were regarded, rightly or wrongly, with implacable suspicion. The elderly and old-fashioned Anglo-Egyptian militarist, with his doctrine and discipline of the barrack-room and the drumhead court-martial, was never regarded by the workers with a shade of suspicion. They simply took him at his word, and the leader of the most turbulent Trades Union element paid to him after his death the simplest tribute in the plainest and most popular language—"He was a straight man." I am so antiquated as to think it a better epitaph than the fashionable phrase about a strong man. Some silent indescribable geniality of fairness in the man once more prevailed against the possibility of passionate misunderstandings, as it had prevailed against the international nervousness of the atmosphere of Fashoda or the tragic border feud of the Boers. I suspect that it lay largely in the fact that this great Englishman was sufficiently English to guess one thing missed by many more sophisticated people—that the English Trades Unions are very English. For good or evil, they are national; they have very little in common with the more international Socialism of the Continent, and nothing whatever in common with the pedantic Socialism of Prussia. Understanding his countrymen by instinct, he did not make a parade of efficiency; for the English dislike the symbols of dictatorship much more than dictatorship. They hate the crown and sceptre of the tyrant much more than his tyranny. They have a national tradition which allows of far too much inequality so long as it is softened with a certain camaraderie, and in which even snobs only remember the coronet of a nobleman on condition that he shall himself seem to forget it.

The other matter is much more important. Though the reverse of vivacious, Kitchener was very vital; and he had one unique mark of vitality—that he had not stopped growing. "An oak should not be transplanted at sixty," said the great orator Grattan when he was transferred from the Parliament of Dublin to the Parliament of Westminster. Kitchener was sixty-four when he turned his face westward to the problem of his own country. There clung to him already all the traditional attributes of the oak—its toughness, its angularity, its closeness of grain and ruggedness of outline—when he was uprooted from the Arabian sands and replanted in the remote western island. Yet the oak not only grew green again and put forth new leaves; it was almost as if, as in a legend, it could put forth a new kind of leaves. Kitchener, with all his taciturnity, really began to put forth a new order of ideas. If a change of opinions is unusual in an elderly man, it is almost unknown in an elderly military man. If the hardening of time was felt even by the poetic and emotional Grattan, it would not have been strange if the hardening had been quite hopeless in the rigid and reticent Kitchener. Yet it was not hopeless; and the fact became the spring of much of the national hope. The grizzled martinet from India and Egypt showed a certain power which is in nearly all great men, but of which St. Paul has become the traditional type—the power of being a great convert as well as a great crusader. It is the real power of re-forming an opinion, which is the very opposite of that mere formlessness which we call fickleness. Nor is the comparison to such an example as St. Paul altogether historically disproportionate; for the point upon which this very typical Englishman changed his mind was a point which is now the pivot of the whole future and perhaps of the very existence of Christendom. For many such Englishmen it might almost be called the discovery of Christendom. It can be called with greater precision, and indeed with almost complete precision, the discovery of Russia.

Military bureaucratic systems everywhere have too much tendency to work upon one idea, and there was a time when the military and bureaucratic system of the British in the East worked on the idea of the fear of Russia. It is needless here to explain that sentiment, and useless to explain it away. It was partly a mere tradition from the natural jingoism of the Crimean War; it was partly in itself a tribute to the epic majesty of the Russian march across mysterious Asia to the legendary Chinese Wall. The point here is that it existed; and where there exists such an idea in such military rulers, they very seldom alter their idea. But Kitchener did alter his idea. Not in mere military obedience, but in genuine human reasonableness, he came late in life to see the Russian as the friend and the Prussian as the enemy. In the inevitable division of British ministerial councils about the distribution of British aid and attention he was the one man who stood most enthusiastically, one might say stubbornly, for the supreme importance of munitioning the magnificent Russian defence. He mystified all the English pessimists, in what seemed to them the blackest hour of pessimism, by announcing that Germany had "shot her bolt"; that she had already lost her chance, not by any of the Allied attacks, but by the stupendous skill and valour of that Russian retreat, which was more triumphant than any attack. It is this discovery that marks an epoch; for that great deliverance was not only the victory of Russia, but very specially the victory of the Russians. Never before was there such a war of men against guns—as awful and inspiring to watch as a war of men against demons. Perhaps the duel of a man with a modern gun is more like that between a man and an enormous dragon; nor is there anything on the weaker side save the ultimate and almost metaphysical truth, that a man can make a gun and a gun cannot make a man. It is the man—the Russian soldier and peasant himself—who has emerged like the hero of an epic, and who is now secure for ever from the sophisticated scandal-mongering and the cultured ignorance of the West.

And it is this that lends an epic and almost primeval symbolism to the tragedy of Kitchener's end. Somehow the very fact that it was incomplete as an action makes it more complete as an allegory. English in his very limitations, English in his late emancipation from them, he was setting forth on an eastward journey different indeed from the many eastward journeys of his life. There are many such noble tragedies of travel in the records of his country; it was so, silently without a trace, that the track of Franklin faded in the polar snows or the track of Gordon in the desert sands. But this was an adventure new for such adventurous men—the finding not of strange foes but of friends yet stranger. Many men of his blood and type—simple, strenuous, somewhat prosaic—had threaded their way through some dark continent to add some treasure or territory to the English name. He was seeking what for us his countrymen has long been a dark continent—but which contains a much more noble treasure. The glory of a great people, long hidden from the English by accidents and by lies, lay before him at his journey's end. That journey was never ended. It remains like a mighty bridge, the mightier for being broken, pointing across a chasm, and promising a mightier thoroughfare between the east and west. In that waste of seas beyond the last northern islets where his ship went down one might fancy his spirit standing, a figure frustrated yet prophetic and pointing to the East, whence are the light of the world and the reunion of Christian men.

Note from the Editor

Odin's Library Classics strives to bring you unedited and unabridged works of classical literature. As such, this is the complete and unabridged version of the original English text unless noted. In some instances, obvious typographical errors have been corrected. This is done to preserve the original text as much as possible. The English language has evolved since the writing and some of the words appear in their original form, or at least the most commonly used form at the time. This is done to protect the original intent of the author. If at any time you are unsure of the meaning of a word, please do your research on the etymology of that word. It is important to preserve the history of the English language.

Taylor Anderson

Printed in Great Britain
by Amazon